FACE TO FACE WITH

LEOPARDS

by Beverly and Dereck Joubert

NATIONAL
GEOGRAPHIC
WASHINGTON, D.C.

We've known this leopard, whom we call Legadema, since she was a cub. When she saw her own reflection in my lens, she wanted to play.

FACE TO FACE

Leopards have eyes like honey and teeth like needles. Their whiskers are very sensitive.

It's not easy to come face to face with a leopard. They are usually shy and secretive. But this one was only eight days old when we spotted her. She seemed curious and bold. And back then, she didn't look fierce at all—more like a fat house cat.

My wife, Beverly, and I have been filming and photographing African wildlife for many years. We were in the Okavango Delta, in Botswana, when we first saw this leopard baby.

As we admired the cub, her mother looked up and

bared her teeth at us. She arched her back and came toward us. We were sitting in our jeep, which doesn't have any doors. They get in the way when we're filming. Now I wondered if that was such a good idea!

Growling, the mother leopard smelled the front of the vehicle. When she came around to my side, our eyes met. Her mouth was full of foamy spit and needle-sharp teeth. I froze. She hissed. Then she turned and went back to her cub. For the next four years, Beverly and I followed that cub as she grew up. The mother leopard never hissed at us again.

About three months later, a thunderstorm broke out while the cub's mother was out hunting. Alone, the cub shivered with fear. It was her first storm. Suddenly, lightning struck the tree next to us.

I thought the cub would run away. But instead, she ran straight toward us and crouched by my feet! After that, people started calling her Legadema (pronounced LACH-ah-DEE-ma). In the local language of Botswana, that means "light from above," or lightning.

Legadema became a kind of friend to us. But we kept our distance. It can be dangerous for leopards and humans to get too close.

MEET

THE LEOPARD

One day Legadema was in a curious mood. She had been watching us as we worked in the jeep. When Beverly moved to the back of the car, Legadema came up to the vehicle. Then she climbed into Beverly's seat and looked me right in the face!

We were amazed, but we knew we had to discourage this behavior. It could be a disaster if Legadema tried it with tourists visiting the game reserve. I decided to teach her some manners the same way her mother would. I hissed at her. She

As the mother leopard licks her cub, she protects the cub from infection. The mom's spit, or saliva, is like an antiseptic.

ignored me. Then I turned on the car heater, which made a more impressive noise. That made her leave.

Legadema is unusual. Most leopards avoid humans, although some have been known to attack and kill people. But usually these big cats prefer other prey, such as antelope and deer.

Leopards are solitary animals. This means they spend most of their lives alone. Except for mating, they avoid other leopards. It's rare to see more than one leopard at a time unless it is a mother and cubs.

Leopard cubs stay with their mothers for about two years. They have a lot to learn in that time. They watch their mothers hunt. They learn which trees are best to hide in and which trunks are easy to climb.

One day, Legadema's mom brought her a present. It was an impala, a type of antelope. Legadema played with it by chasing it and pouncing on it. This game helped her practice the hunting skills she would need to survive on her own one day.

When Legadema was about 13 months old, her mother chased her away. The young leopard had been killing her own food for a while, so her mom must have known she was ready. Legadema wandered around by herself, touching and sniffing each of her mother's favorite trees. She hunted small animals. Her mother seemed to give her some space in their territory. We think she may even have been watching over Legadema and keeping in touch by scent and markings rather than by actually meeting.

⬆ *When cats lift their young, the cubs freeze. You probably shouldn't wriggle too much when mom's sharp teeth are around your neck!*

A sausage tree provides the perfect fortress for Legadema and her mom. It has lots of deep holes to hide in, and the cub can dig her claws in its soft bark and climb.

After a hard night of hunting, mom just wants to rest, but Legadema has other ideas.

Over time, Legadema found her place in the leopard world as an adult. Now she, too, is a mother.

But she hasn't forgotten us. We had been away for a while and then went back for a visit. As soon as Legadema spotted us, she came over to the car. She looked up into Beverly's eyes. Then she circled over to me and sniffed my shoe. Soon she was lying in the shade under our jeep, just like she used to.

Leopards catch their prey off guard by leaping to the ground from high up in the trees.

FOREST GHOSTS

Leopards prowl the forest like ghosts. They slip through the shadows. They slink through tall grass. Even in bright sunlight, it's hard to see them. Their yellowish fur with dark spots blends into the background. This helps them hide from their prey until they are ready to pounce.

Like all big cats, leopards are predators. This means they hunt, kill, and eat other animals to survive. Leopards eat almost anything they can

This vervet monkey was just a little too slow and couldn't escape a sly leopard.

15

catch, from birds to monkeys to Cape buffalo. Almost nothing is safe!

The leopard hunts alone. It creeps up on its prey secretly and silently. This is called stalking. We have watched a leopard lie in wait for hours, watching an antelope nibble grass. Slowly, the

⬇ A leopard's powerful jaw muscles and sharp claws help it drag an impala up a tree, away from other predators that might steal it.

powerful cat inches closer and closer, until—*wham!* It springs at its prey, pins the animal down, and kills it, usually with one fierce bite.

Instead of eating their catch on the spot, leopards often drag it away. They do this to get away from the lions and hyenas that might steal their meal. They stash it under a bush or haul it up into the treetops. A leopard is so strong that it can drag an animal twice its weight up a tree. It does this with the help of its powerful neck, shoulder, and jaw muscles and its strong legs.

Besides being good climbers, leopards are also strong swimmers. They will catch and eat fish, crabs, and other water animals—even small hippos!

Leopards have sharp eyesight and keen hearing, which help them detect prey. They usually hunt at night. But at Mombo, the region in the Okavango Delta where Legadema lives, we saw her hunt during the day and night.

To us it looks like leopards really have fun sometimes. An adult leopard might spot a squirrel and spend an hour chasing it up and down trees, over logs, and in and out of holes. I think the big cat must enjoy the chase, since

⬆ *Predators eat meat, and they have to kill in order to survive. Predators and prey are a natural part of life in the wild.*

CAN A LEOPARD CHANGE HIS SPOTS?

Telling one leopard from another seems hard. Here are some ways researchers "spot" the difference!

— On the fat upper lip on either side of a leopard's nose are rows of dark black spots with a whisker coming out of each. The pattern of these whisker spots is different for each cat.

— Every leopard also has a unique pattern of dark spots around its neck. This band of black spots is called a necklace. In addition, researchers often use the spots on the sides of leopards' bodies to identify them.

— As a cub, Legadema had a unique spot on her upper lip that was a perfect way to identify her. She still has it today, which shows that a leopard really does not change its spots!

the small mouthful of fur doesn't seem like much of a reward for all that effort.

Sometimes leopards stalk and prey on baboons. But sometimes the baboons are the predators. When Legadema was a cub, we saw a troop of baboons try to drag her and her mother out of their den. A mob of baboons can rip a leopard to shreds. Legadema learned to hide or run away when she met a group of them. Lions also pose a danger to leopards. We have seen lions chase a leopard up into a tree and then try to pull it down and kill it.

Smell is important to leopards. They claw tree trunks and spray their urine on trees to leave their scent behind. This tells other leopards that the territory is theirs. This way, they can avoid others. If one leopard does see another, it will usually turn away. Leopards also roar to let other leopards know where they are. A leopard's roar sounds sort of like a deep, raspy cough.

Leopards live in many parts of Africa and Asia. A few leopards appear to be solid black. I once saw one for an instant. Within the black coat there were even darker spots, like a normal leopard has. This is

⬆ Legadema makes a quick exit when she spots these elephants looming over her.

different from what is commonly known as a black panther, which is often a black jaguar or even a dark mountain lion. No matter what their overall color is, leopards are expert at disappearing. It's almost as if they have Harry Potter's invisibility cloak! 🐾

Legadema scans the tree-tops for squirrels. Hunting them became an obsession for her.

LEOPARD LEGACY

As a cub, Legadema loved to play. She just had to watch out for her mom's sharp teeth and claws—and that cat breath!

Leopards live in more climates and habitats than any other big cat. They live in Africa, Central Asia, India, Russia, and China. They live in forests, grasslands, deserts, and mountains. They survive in warm climates and in cold. In fact, leopards can adapt to nearly any habitat. In some parts of the world, they even live in sub-urban areas. They just need a place to hide in and hunt.

But even though they are very adaptable, they still face many problems. One of the biggest is habitat loss. As human populations grow, we take over land that

➡ *When there are baboons in the area, Legadema returns to a safe place.*

HOW TO SPOT A BIG CAT BY ITS SPOTS

Leopards aren't the only big cats with spots. Jaguars and cheetahs have them, too. Here's how to spot the difference.

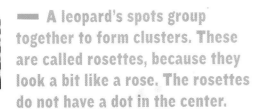

— A leopard's spots group together to form clusters. These are called rosettes, because they look a bit like a rose. The rosettes do not have a dot in the center.

— The jaguar's coat is patterned with rings of small black spots. The rings are also called rosettes. They often have a black dot in the center.

— The spots on a cheetah's coat are solid. They are evenly spaced and do not form rosettes.

was once wild, and the animals lose their habitat.

When leopards live near human settlements, they may prey on dogs and on livestock such as cattle and pigs. To protect their animals, farmers shoot, trap, or poison the big cats. In some places, wildlife conservation groups pay cattle owners for livestock that leopards kill, as long as the owners don't kill the cats.

Leopards face another challenge. Some African countries still allow leopard hunting. Leopards are hunted for their valuable fur coats. They are also killed for their tails, claws, and whiskers, which are used in some traditional medicines.

Permits are issued, allowing only a certain number of leopards to be hunted worldwide. But we think it's

⬆ *She's fully grown now, but we can usually still find Legadema in the same trees she liked to climb as a cub.*

still too many, because no one knows how many are killed by poachers, who hunt illegally, without permits.

Leopards are very difficult to see, let alone count, but we know their numbers are declining. Today, some conservationists think there may be as few as 50,000 mature leopards, but we need more information. In some parts of the world, especially Asia,

Legadema perches confidently on a branch, queen of all she surveys.

the leopard is already on the verge of extinction.

Leopards play an important role in the wild. Without the top predators, the number of prey species would go out of balance. There would be so many prey animals that soon they would have trouble finding food. They would damage the environment by eating too much plant life. So predators are important to the balance of nature. They prey on the weaker members of a herd, making the herd stronger. They keep them on the move, fit and alert, always ready to flee from those spots in the grass that just might be a leopard in disguise.

Today, many people are turning against hunting, and many national parks protect the big cats. Tourism also helps by raising money for conservation and helping people appreciate wildlife. We are very hopeful that in time more people will learn to value these precious animals and that their populations will start to recover.

HOW YOU CAN HELP

▼ *Leopards have keen eyesight.*

■ Helping leopards starts with understanding them. Learn all you can about these big cats. You are already off to a good start! Read about leopards in books and magazines and on the Internet. Watch documentary films and TV programs about them. Visit leopards in zoos. The more you learn about leopards, the more you will appreciate them. You might even come to love them as deeply as we do.

■ Talk to everyone you can about leopards and share what you've learned. Someone who is passionate about something and who knows a lot about the subject can have a lot of influence.

■ Support conservation groups that protect big cats. For example, the World Wildlife Fund and the African Wildlife Foundation have up-to-date information on leopard conservation on their Web sites. So does the National Geographic Big Cat Initiative, which we founded. It raises funds for emergency help for lions, leopards, cheetahs, and tigers. And it is working. A few years ago, when we started the program, one area in Kenya was losing 40 lions a year and countless leopards. A year later, the program had helped limit the losses to just one lion and no leopards at all.

■ Think about how to raise money to help conservation organizations keep big cats safe. Rally your classmates, teachers, friends, and families. Encourage them to go on the Web site of one of these groups and donate whatever they can afford. Every little bit helps to keep these cats from dying out.

■ You can help preserve the world's wild places for leopards and other wildlife by doing what you can to reduce the impact you have on the natural world each day. Don't waste water. Recycle whatever you can. The fewer forests that are chopped down to make paper products, for example, the more space there will be for all wildlife to survive.

IT'S YOUR TURN

Not everyone gets the chance to see leopards face to face in the wild. Fortunately, several zoos have leopard exhibits where you can watch the great cats firsthand. But to get a sense of what it's like to track leopards in the wild, you don't have to go any farther than a local park or your own backyard. Like the forests of Africa, these places are telling a wonderful tale. You just need to pay attention.

1 Listen. We find many leopards just by listening to the other animals. Calling birds, screeching squirrels, and screaming monkeys all sound the alarm when a leopard is nearby. The next time you're outside, listen to what's going on. If the birds suddenly start squawking, there could be a cat slinking along nearby.

2 Watch closely. All cats like to hide, whether they're hundred-pound leopards or eight-pound house cats. It's the way they stalk and hunt. Sometimes, if we keep looking at the spot the birds are showing us, we suddenly see a beautiful pair of amber eyes looking back. In the park or yard, you might spot a pair of cat eyes peering out from the bushes.

3 Move slowly. Never move directly at the cat. To cats, fast approaches are rude. And if you don't know the cat, do not get too close! Leave the way you came, slowly and quietly.

Happy tracking!

Legadema lounges lazily on a tree limb.

FACTS AT A GLANCE

⬇ *Legadema and her mom patrolling their territory.*

Scientific Name
Leopards belong to the cat family, called Felidae. The species name is *Panthera pardus.*

Common Name
There are several different varieties, or subspecies, of leopards. Some are named after the place they come from, such as the Chinese leopard, which lives in northern China. Despite their names, the snow leopard *(Panthera uncia)* and the clouded leopard *(Neofelis nebulosa)* are not true leopards.

Lifespan
In the wild, leopards live 12 to 17 years. In captivity they have been known to live 23 years.

Size
Leopards weigh 66 to 176 pounds (30 to 80 kg). Males are heavier than females. Leopards vary in length from 3 to 6 feet (91 to 191 cm); tails are about 23 to 44 inches (58 to 110 cm) long.

Diet
Leopards are meat eaters, or carnivores. They eat a wide variety of animals, including antelope, deer, squirrels and other rodents, birds, monkeys, baboons, fish, reptiles, and porcupines. We have seen them kill 33 species of wildlife in the area of Africa that we study. Leopards also will eat meat killed by other animals. I've even seen a leopard eating an elephant! One day some lions were eating an old elephant when a male leopard snuck in quietly and joined the feast.

Reproduction
Females are pregnant for about 3½ months before they give birth. They usually have litters of two to three cubs. Life as a baby leopard can be tough. Legadema's mother lost five previous cubs to hyenas, baboons, and other predators before Legadema was born.

Habitat and Range
These adaptable cats live in a wide variety of habitats—rain forests, open woodlands, dry grasslands, plains, deserts, and mountains. They can survive in cold and warm climates. They live in sub-Saharan Africa,

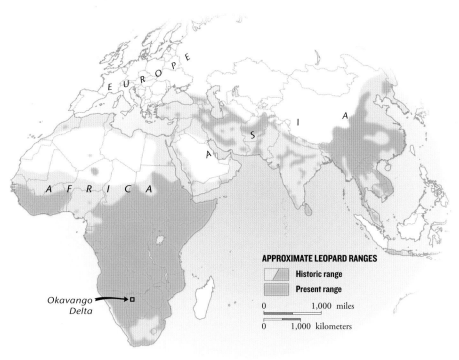

APPROXIMATE LEOPARD RANGES

Historic range

Present range

0   1,000 miles

0   1,000 kilometers

Okavango Delta

As the map shows, leopards were once more widely distributed throughout the world than they are today.

northeast Africa, the Arabian Peninsula, the Middle East, Central Asia, India, and China.

Biggest Threats

Loss of habitat is one of the biggest threats to leopards' survival. Their habitats are being destroyed for logging and farming and to make way for roads and houses. Leopards are also being shot, trapped, or poisoned by farmers who believe the big cats are killing their livestock.

Hunters and poachers kill the big cats for sport or for their fur and other body parts.

Status in the Wild

The number of leopards living in the wild has declined greatly in the last hundred years, and it continues to decrease. Today, some conservationists estimate that about 50,000 mature leopards exist in the wild. While they are still fairly numerous in some places, such as parts of

southern Africa, in other places leopards are endangered.

The rarest leopard of all is probably the Amur leopard. It was once found throughout the Korea Peninsula, northeastern China, and southeastern Russia. Now it is extinct in South Korea. Only a handful of Amur leopards are left in the mountainous regions of China and Russia. Researchers estimate that there are fewer than 50 of them living in the wild today.

GLOSSARY

Adapt: To become suited to one's surroundings. Animals can adapt to changes in the environment over many generations.

Endangered: A species with very few individuals remaining. If the number of individuals rises, the classification may change to "threatened" or "recovered." If the number falls, the species may become "extinct," meaning no individuals are left.

Habitat: The local environment in which an animal lives.

Livestock: Animals such as cattle, pigs, or sheep that are kept and raised by humans.

Poacher: A person who takes or kills an animal illegally.

Predator: An animal that hunts, kills, and then feeds on other animals.

Prey: An animal that is hunted for food.

Range: The area in which an animal lives.

Species: A group of animals or plants that look similar, can breed with one another, and have offspring who can also breed successfully.

Stalk: To hunt or track secretly and quietly.

Territory: An area that an animal, or a group of animals, lives in and defends from other animals of the same species.

FIND OUT MORE

Books & Articles

Gamble, Cyndi, and Rodney Griffiths. *Leopards.* Voyageur Press, 2004.

Joubert, Dereck, and Beverly Joubert. *Eye of the Leopard.* National Geographic, 2009.

Joubert, Dereck. "Lessons of the Hunt." *National Geographic* magazine, April 2007.

Sunquist, Mel, and Fiona Sunquist. *Wild Cats of the World.* University of Chicago Press, 2002.

Films

Eye of the Leopard. National Geographic, 2006. Not rated.

Watch short videos on big cats at http://video.nationalgeographic.com/video/player/animals/mammals-animals/cats/leopard_lifecycle.html.

Web Sites

Get the latest stats on big cats and how you can help protect them at Big Cat Initiative: http://www.bigcatinitiative.com/

Meet the leopard and many other animals in the Wildlife Gallery at the African Wildlife Foundation: http://www.awf.org/section/wildlife/gallery. You will also find news on conservation projects.

Listen to a leopard at the San Diego Zoo's Web site at http://www.sandiegozoo.org/animalbytes/t-leopard.html.

Check out the leopard pages at National Geographic online: http://animals.nationalgeographic.com/animals/mammals/leopard.html

Play some big cat games at http://www.predatorconservation.com/kids.htm

RESEARCH & PHOTOGRAPHIC NOTES

Researching and working in one of the world's most beautiful places is like a dream come true. And for us, a day spent tracking a tiny leopard cub is a perfect day. Each day we find ourselves snapping awake in the dark, usually around 4 o'clock in the morning, eager to get out and find her. We tumble out of bed, pull on clothes already laid out the night before, shake out shoes in case any scorpions have crawled in, and shove all our stuff into steel trunks so the mice don't get in. Then we zip the tent closed behind us, to stop baboons or monkeys from sneaking in and stealing our things. Nowadays, we have to double lock the zippers because they have become so clever!

Then we head out in our jeep. Beverly stands up through a roof hatch, searching, listening to the forest, while I scan the track ahead for the slightest shape of footprints or a movement in the brush.

Legadema has favorite trees to lie in, so we check those. Once we find her, that's it for us for the day. What she does, we do.

Our vehicle is our office, so we keep a lot of cameras spread around, ready for action. We have a section for food, books, journals, hot water for tea, and cold water for the midday heat—which can reach 130 degrees. There is a mosquito net that we couldn't live without. Hats, sunscreen, sunglasses, night glasses for driving when the bugs are out, a sound recorder, and microphones that can pick up a leopard panting at 50 yards. We also have sleeping bags—sometimes in winter it can go below freezing at night.

Our vehicle is our best friend, just as a horse is a cowboy's best friend. Sadly, I don't treat it very well. I drive it in places where no vehicle is meant to go—into valleys of mud that people can't walk through, over rocks to the tops of hills, and across rivers so deep the water comes up over my belt as I sit driving.

This kind of life is not for everyone. But for people who want adventure, it's the best life there is.

—DJ & BJ

TO THE 10,000 LEOPARDS
THAT HAVE GIVEN THEIR LIVES
TO THE VANITY OF MAN SINCE
WE FIRST MET LEGADEMA, AND
THE COUNTLESS NUMBER FALLEN
TO THE POACHERS GUNS ... AND
TO A LITTLE LEOPARD WITH
MISCHIEF IN HER EYES.

—DJ & BJ

Acknowledgments

We looked into the eyes of one little leopard one day and our lives were changed forever. She stole our hearts in a way that makes our hearts swell. We developed a trust with her that very few humans even have with another human being. I have seldom been in the company of such greatness in one character, or such beauty and it is a leopard. The other more enduring beauty in my life is Beverly, as rare a creature as a leopard, and I have to thank both of these wonderous females. We mutually thank the country and citizens of Botswana for keeping spaces enough to house these phantoms of the forest.

—Dereck and Beverly Joubert

The publisher wishes to thank Dr. Andrew Stein, Research Coordinator of the Predator Conservation Trust, for his review of the map and text. For their important contributions on leopard distribution for the map, we thank Chris and Tilde Stuart, Rachel Ikemeh, and Farid Belbachir. Arezoo Sanei contributed information from her 2008 work, *Analysis of leopard* (Panthera pardus) *status in Iran* (No. 1). Tehran: Sepeher Publication Center. Second edition. P. 71.

Page 22 center left by Steve Winter/ National GeographicStock.com; page 22 bottom left by Andrew Dowsett/iStock Photo.com. Back cover photograph by Corly and Arjen Vons.

Published by the National Geographic Society

John M. Fahey, Jr., *President and Chief Executive Officer*

Gilbert M. Grosvenor, *Chairman of the Board*

Tim T. Kelly, *President, Global Media Group*

John Q. Griffin, *President, Publishing*

Nina D. Hoffman, *Executive Vice President; President, Book Publishing Group*

Staff for This Book

Nancy Laties Feresten, *Vice President, Editor-in-Chief of Children's Books*

Bea Jackson, *Design and Illustrations Director, Children's Books*

Amy Shields, *Executive Editor*

Mary Beth Oelkers-Keegan, *Project Editor*

David M. Seager, *Art Director*

Lori Renda, *Illustrations Editor*

M.F. Delano, *Researcher*

Carl Mehler, *Director of Maps*

Sven M. Dolling, *Cartographic Editor*

Jennifer Thornton, *Managing Editor*

Grace Hill, *Associate Managing Editor*

R. Gary Colbert, *Production Director*

Lewis R. Bassford, *Production Manager*

Nicole Elliott, *Manufacturing Manager*

Susan Borke, *Legal and Business Affairs*

Front cover & pages 2–3: Face to face with a young leopard; *front flap:* Legadema shows off her sharp teeth; *back cover:* Beverly and Dereck Joubert at work in Africa's Okavango Delta, Botswana; *page one:* A leopard lazily lounging on a limb.

Library of Congress Cataloging-in-Publication Data

Joubert, Dereck.
 Face to face with leopards / by Dereck Joubert and Beverly Joubert.
   p. cm.
 Includes bibliographical references and index.
 ISBN 978-1-4263-0636-5 (hardcover : alk. paper) -- ISBN 978-1-4263-0637-2 (library binding : alk. paper)
 1. Leopard--Juvenile literature. I. Joubert, Beverly. II. Title.
 QL737.C23J687 2009
 599.75'54--dc22

                20090114

Founded in 1888, the National Geographic Society is one of the largest nonprofit scientific and educational organizations in the world. It reaches more than 285 million people worldwide each month through its official journal, NATIONAL GEOGRAPHIC, and its four other magazines; the National Geographic Channel; television documentaries; radio programs; films; books; videos and DVDs; maps; and interactive media. National Geographic has funded more than 8,000 scientific research projects and supports an education program combating geographic illiteracy.

For more information, please call 1-800-NGS LINE (647-5463) or write to the following address:

National Geographic Society
1145 17th Street N.W.
Washington, D.C. 20036-4688 U.S.A.

Visit us online at www.nationalgeographic.org/books. Librarians and teachers, visit us at www.ngchildrensbooks.org. Kids and parents, visit us at kids.nationalgeographic.com.

For information about special discounts for bulk purchases, please contact National Geographic Books Special Sales: ngspecsales@ngs.org. For rights or permissions inquiries, please contact National Geographic Books Subsidiary Rights: ngbookrights@ngs.org.

Printed in China
09/RRDS/1

Book design by David M. Seager. The body text of the book is set in ITC Century. The display text is set in Knockout and Party Noid.